UNFINISHED
STUDY GUIDE

BELIEVING

IS ONLY THE BEGINNING

UNFINISHED

STUDY GUIDE

SIX SESSIONS

RICHARD STEARNS

with DIXON KINSER

THOMAS NELSON

Since 1798

NASHVILLE   DALLAS   MEXICO CITY   RIO DE JANEIRO

Published in Nashville, Tennessee, by Thomas Nelson. Thomas Nelson is a registered trademark of Thomas Nelson, Inc.

Author is represented by the literary agency of Alive Communications, Inc., 7680 Goddard Street, Suite 200, Colorado Springs, CO 80920. www.alivecommunications.com

Thomas Nelson, Inc. titles may be purchased in bulk for educational, business, fund-raising, or sales promotional use. For information, please e-mail SpecialMarkets@ ThomasNelson.com.

At the author's request, all royalties due to the author will benefit World Vision's work with children in need.

ISBN 978-05291-1028-2 (trade paper)
ISBN 978-08499-6041-2 (ebook)

Printed in the United States of America

13 14 15 16 17 RRD 9 8 7 6 5 4 3 2 1

CONTENTS

Introduction 7
How to Use This Study Guide 9

SESSION 1
THE MEANING OF LIFE AND OTHER
IMPORTANT THINGS 13

SESSION 2
MAGIC KINGDOM, TRAGIC KINGDOM, AND
THE KINGDOM OF GOD 31

SESSION 3
THE INVITATION OF GOD 49

SESSION 4
WE WERE MADE FOR MORE 65

SESSION 5
SPIRITUAL DOMINOES 79

SESSION 6
GOD'S GREAT ADVENTURE FOR YOUR LIFE 95

Group Leader Notes 111

INTRODUCTION

"Jesus did not call us to build an institution; he called us
to lead a revolution."

(*Unfinished*, p. 175)

WELCOME TO *UNFINISHED*! Over the next six weeks you will be invited to discover your life's purpose by joining God in nothing less than changing the world. Does that sound audacious? It should. The plan is God's. But what's more daring is God's desire to use people like you and me to get the job done.

It is for this reason that this study and the book on which it is based are called *Unfinished*. The name carries two meanings. First, "unfinished" echoes back to the ascension, when Jesus left the task of building God's kingdom to his disciples. He had begun the work, but at the time of his ascension, that task remained incomplete. So Jesus instructed his followers to "go and make disciples of all nations, baptizing them in the name of the Father and of the Son and of the Holy Spirit" (Matthew 28:19). The very DNA of the church includes a charge to finish the job Jesus has given us.

This leads to the second meaning of the word "unfinished," which is more personal. Each of us has a specific, God-given role to play in fulfilling Jesus' instructions. We were all made for a reason. However, until we embrace the role the Creator has given us to play in his great story of redemption, we too will remain "unfinished." This study explores how both of these "unfinished" items can find their completion at the same time when we accept Jesus' invitation to become his disciples.

7

That being said, accepting Jesus' invitation to discipleship is not something we can do alone. We will necessarily need a community. Therefore, your *Unfinished* experience will be anchored in weekly small group interaction. A small group is an excellent place to process the content of this study, ask questions, and learn from others as you listen to what God is doing in their lives. If you are new to small groups, know that they can be a deeply rewarding time of intimacy and friendship. However, they can also be a disaster. Keeping the following ground rules in mind will make this group experience a fruitful one for everyone involved.

First, work to make the group a safe place. That means being honest about your thoughts and feelings as well as listening carefully to everyone else's. Second, resist the temptation to "fix" a problem someone might be having or to correct someone else's theology. That's not what this time is for. Third, and finally, keep everything your group shares confidential. All this will foster a rewarding sense of community in your *Unfinished* study group and give God's Spirit a powerful forum to heal, challenge, and send you all out to finish the job.

HOW TO USE
THIS STUDY GUIDE

BECAUSE THIS STUDY is based on the book *Unfinished* by Rich Stearns, participants are invited to do some pre-reading prior to each group gathering. Directions for this reading can be found in the highlighted "Pre-Session Personal Study" section at the beginning of each session. Each pre-session activity will direct you to the chapters of the book that correspond with that week's video study. The reading is meant to complement your engagement with the video; the quotes and questions are designed to help you process what you are learning. For this reason, each participant is strongly encouraged to get a copy of the book *Unfinished* and read ahead to get the most out of his or her study experience.

During your group time, you will watch a video clip where Rich Stearns (author of the book and president of World Vision U.S.) takes you into the core content of *Unfinished*. The video will be followed each week by a time of small group discussion. There are a number of questions available for this time, but do not feel like you have to get through all of them. Your leader will focus on the ones that resonate with your group and guide you from there.

The last two elements of each session are practical experiments designed to challenge you and your study group to actually act on what you have been learning. The group portion (called "Doing the Word") is to be completed during your meeting time, while the individual portion (called "Living the Word" and highlighted the same as the pre-session material) is to be completed on your own. Use your study guide to record what you are learning during the "Living the Word" activities, because starting in session two, time is provided to check in about the previous week's activity. During this check-in time, you will be asked to share your experiences as well as listen to those of your fellow group members. However, don't worry if you could not do the experiment one week or are just joining the study. Hearing what others have learned will be nourishment enough on its own.

Now you are ready to enter the world of *Unfinished*. This is a study that has the potential to change your life—if you let it. Be honest about where you are struggling and resist the temptation to shut down if the content hits close to home. Examining our lives and admitting where they are out of sync or inconsistent takes courage, but it is not an invitation to shame. Instead, it is actually a way to open our hearts to God's love. Knowing this love is what Jesus' commission is all about, because knowing this love changes everything. And if we seek it, Jesus promises, that is exactly what we will find.

If you are a group leader, there are additional resources for you in the back of this guide.

SPECIAL NOTE

OVER THE NEXT six weeks you will be immersed in the hope and challenge of Rich Stearns's *Unfinished*. The meaning and significance of your journey can be even greater if you take time to complete the "Pre-Session Personal Study" that is highlighted at the beginning of every session. This activity will introduce you to the content of the *Unfinished* book and prepare you to more fully participate in the *Unfinished* small group experience.

THE MEANING OF LIFE AND OTHER IMPORTANT THINGS

"The meaning, purpose, and significance of our lives are found only by aligning our lives with God's purposes, in lives committed to following Jesus Christ."

(*Unfinished*, p. xviii)

PRE-SESSION PERSONAL STUDY

Based on the introduction and chapters 1–2 of the Unfinished *book*

INTRODUCTION

Read the introduction to *Unfinished* (pp. xvii–xxiii); then meditate on the following quotes and answer the related questions. (This same basic format will repeat in each pre-session of the guide. Use the space provided or a separate notebook to record your responses.)

> "So why is it that so many Christians seem to lack that sense of fullness of life? They go to church, read their Bibles, and say their prayers but still feel that something is missing." *(p. xviii)*

Do you ever feel something is missing from your life? If so, when do you feel that way? Why do you feel that way?

How would you answer the question posed in the quote if someone asked you?

"Our Christian faith is not just a way to find forgiveness for sin in order to enter eternal life, yet it is that. It is not just a system of right beliefs about ultimate truth and the order of things, though it is that. Nor is it just a way to find God's comfort in times of trouble or a helpful code of conduct for how to live a good and productive life, though it is those things too. Fundamentally, the Christian faith is a call to leave everything else behind, follow our Lord and Savior Jesus Christ, and join in the great mission of Christ in our world. It is a call to forsake all else and follow him. Only then will we become completed people — people living according to God's deepest purpose for our lives." *(p. xviii)*

How do you experience this quote from *Unfinished*? Does it inspire you? Make you angry?

What would it mean for you to leave everything behind?

What are you most afraid to leave behind?

> "Listen carefully to these next few statements: You don't have to go to the Congo or to Uzbekistan to change the world. You don't have to be brilliant to change the world — or wealthy or influential or a spiritual giant. But you do have to say yes to the invitation." *(p. xxii)*

Can you change the world for God's kingdom right where you are?

What does it mean to say yes to the invitation? What will saying yes require of you?

Does a quote like this sound like good news? Why or why not?

CHAPTER 1: THE MEANING OF LIFE AND OTHER IMPORTANT THINGS

Read *Unfinished* chapter 1 (pp. 1–16).

Pick one quote or concept that really connected with you from today's reading and write it down to share, as appropriate, with the group during session one.

> "I want to suggest to you that our lives are part of a much bigger story—one that began in eternity and one that will continue indefinitely into the future. And unless we understand how our story fits into this bigger story, we will live our lives with little sense of real purpose or significance, drifting through life like a ship without a rudder." *(pp. 6–7)*

Do you know someone with a real sense of purpose? What is he or she like?

Do you feel like your life has purpose? Why or why not? Does your answer have anything to do with your Christianity? Why or why not?

What does it mean to you that God has a purpose for your life?

CHAPTER 2: GOD'S BIG STORY

Read *Unfinished* chapter 2 (pp. 17–30).

At the end of the chapter Rich retells the entire biblical narrative. Have you ever heard the story told the way he does? How did you experience his version? What are the implications for our lives when the story is told this way?

> "I came to believe that the most plausible explanation for the universe was that God was real and he had created all that we see; that there was a painter behind this incredible painting, an author behind this astonishing story. I also came to believe that Jesus of Nazareth was indeed God incarnate—that God had taken human form in order to inaugurate a new and deeper kind of relationship with us." *(pp. 19–20)*

In this section of the book, Rich shares his experience of coming to faith in Jesus. What was your experience of coming to faith? How was it similar or different from Rich's?

"The truth is that the only things we can really know about God are the things he has chosen to reveal to us in one way or another. We can discern things about God from observing what he created. When we see the world around us, we see vastness, complexity, power, order, beauty, creativity, precision, and majesty. And all of these words say something about the Creator."   *(p. 23)*

What are three adjectives you would use to describe God? Why did you pick the words you did?

What does the creation itself tell us about the great Creator?

GROUP STUDY

INTRODUCTION

One of the subplots in the 2003 movie *Finding Nemo* is about of a group of fish who long to live in the ocean but are trapped in a dentist's aquarium. They can see the harbor from their prison in the dentist's office, but no matter how many escape plans they devise, they can never quite get there. Finally they succeed. As the last of the group plops into the sea, the newly freed fish silently take stock of their situation: they're floating in individual plastic bags in the midst of a vast harbor, with no tools or opposable thumbs with which to get out of the bags. After a moment, one of them humorously asks the obvious question, "Now what?"

"Now what?" indeed.

"Now what?" is a question many Christians find themselves asking after they make an initial commitment to Jesus. They truly love God and have a sincere belief in Jesus, but they sense something missing. They wonder what they are supposed to do next. Is there more to this life of faith than simply going to church, praying, reading the Bible, and waiting to die? The answer to this question is a resounding yes!

Over the last century, American Christianity has become hyperfocused on believing the right things. We have produced thousands of theology books, used countless bytes on the Internet defending our religious particulars, and even left old churches to start new ones based on differences in doctrine. But what if belief is only half the story? Yes, it is important to trust God and believe in Jesus, but that is only the first step. What comes next is just as important but also much harder: actually doing what Jesus commands. Over and over again, Jesus insists that his followers and friends are the ones who both "hear" and "do" the things he teaches (Luke 6:49; John 15:14). Which brings us back to that very important question from *Finding Nemo*: "Now what?"

Chances are you are engaged in this study because you are interested in Jesus. You believe in him and trust him as Lord and Savior, but you want to know more about how to live out your faith. You know that Jesus has things to say about the way we prioritize our time and what we do with our money. You know that God expects his worshipers to have a particular relationship with the poor and people in need. You know that God's agenda is for the renewal of all things, but you wonder how your life fits into that big plan. If this is the case, then you have come to the right place.

These kinds of questions are questions about story. They ask what kind of story God has been and is still telling in this world. They ask who the main characters of that story are and, more personally, how each of our individual stories fits into God's big one. They ask what is the ultimate purpose and meaning of life. And that is why it is such good news that we wonder about these things, because such wonderings come from a place of hope. Hope that things can be different. Hope that God has not abandoned this world but is indeed rescuing it. And hope that the significance, satisfaction, and peace we long for are not actually found in the pursuit of money, sex, or power but in something far more exciting. However, pursuing the answers takes courage and intentionality. Jesus is inviting you to join him on this journey of discipleship. Do you want to accept that invitation?

CHECKING IN

After welcome time, briefly share highlights of your pre-session reading. Then answer this question:

If God could do one thing in your life during this study, what would you want it to be?

HEARING THE WORD

Read Matthew 7:24–27 out loud twice in the group. If possible, use two different readers. Then answer the questions that follow.

"Therefore everyone who hears these words of mine and puts them into practice is like a wise man who built his house on the rock. The rain came down, the streams rose, and the winds blew and beat against that house; yet it did not fall, because it had its foundation on the rock. But everyone who hears these words of mine and does not put them into practice is like a foolish man who built his house on sand. The rain came down, the streams rose, and the winds blew and beat against that house, and it fell with a great crash."

What word or phrase stuck out to you most when the Scripture was read?

Why do you think Jesus uses the metaphor of a house in his teaching?

WATCH THE VIDEO

Watch the session one video clip, using the space below to take notes. When the video ends, take a moment to jot down one or two things that you learned, disagreed with, or were surprised by.

VIDEO DISCUSSION

First Impressions

1. Before everyone shares in the large group, turn to one or two people next to you and finish this sentence, "After watching the video clip, one question I now have is . . ."

Community Reflection

2. As a group, summarize why Rich says the book is called *Unfinished*. Why is this concept a challenge to the church today?

3. How do you define the "meaning of life"? Does your life and lifestyle match up with your definition? Why or why not?

4. Rich says that "truth matters" and that "truth has consequences." What do you think this means? Do you think there is any such thing as truth? Why or why not? Where does your definition of "truth" come from?

5. In the video, Rich suggests that there are three ways to answer the question, "What is the meaning of life?" The first option is that there is no meaning to life and everything is purposeless and random. The second option is that life only has the meaning we want it to have. Here we make up our own code of ethics and hold that what's true for me may not be true for you. The third option is that we decide to become part of God's story and find our purpose in his will for our lives.

Do you like these categories? Do they work, in your opinion? Did any of them particularly resonate with you? Did any of them not? Why did you answer the way you did?

Which of the three options best describe how you are finding your meaning in life right now?

6. God has invited us to join him in changing the world. Does this sound like good news to you? Why or why not? Are there any places in your life you think you might already be joining God? Are there any places where you know you are not joining God? Explain.

EXPLORING THE WORD

Reread Matthew 7:24–27 as a group.

Does the text sound different to you now? Why or why not?

Jesus says that the wise person hears his words and puts them into practice. Are there any of Jesus' words that are harder to practice than others?

What is at least one implication of Jesus' words on your life this week?

DOING THE WORD

Jesus' teaching about houses built on either rocks or sand is the conclusion of a much larger sermon. Earlier in that same sermon Jesus instructed those who call him Lord to do the following:

"You have heard that it was said, 'Love your neighbor and hate your enemy.' But I tell you, love your enemies and pray for those who persecute you, that you may be children of your Father in heaven."   *(Matthew 5:43–45)*

As part of a group exercise in "doing" Jesus' words, each of you call to mind someone you experience as an enemy or persecutor. Then go around the room and take turns offering a one-word prayer of blessing for that person. The word can be general (like "peace") or something more specific. Afterward, answer these questions:

Was this a hard or easy exercise?

If you prayed for your enemies every day, how do you think it would change you?

Is there a way to pray for your enemies that would "miss Jesus' point"? If so, what would it be?

CLOSING PRAYER

Close the session with this popular version of the prayer Jesus taught his disciples to pray in the Sermon on the Mount (Matthew 6:9–13):

> Our Father in heaven, hallowed be your name,
> your kingdom come, your will be done,
>   on earth as it is in heaven.
> Give us today our daily bread.
> Forgive us our sins
>   as we forgive those who sin against us.
> Save us from the time of trial,
>   and deliver us from evil.
> For the kingdom, the power, and the glory are yours,
>   now and forever. Amen.

PERSONAL ACTIVITY

LIVING THE WORD

Between now and the next session, you are invited to individually *live* one of the words of Jesus.

Jesus says that the whole of the Bible's teaching before him could be summed up in our call to love God with everything we've got and to love our neighbor as ourselves (Matthew 22:37–40). Embody this call by performing one anonymous act of kindness or generosity this week: anything from buying a stranger lunch to emptying the dishwasher without being asked. Whatever you do, do it with intention and love and not for any credit.

Write about your experience below so that you can briefly share about it during the check-in portion of session two.

What did you choose to do?

What was your experience like?

MAGIC KINGDOM, TRAGIC KINGDOM, AND THE KINGDOM OF GOD

"Christ did not call us to retreat from the world's pain but to enter it. He called us to go."

(*Unfinished*, p. 54)

PRE-SESSION PERSONAL STUDY

Based on chapters 3–5 of the Unfinished *book*

CHAPTER 3: WHY DID JESUS LEAVE?

Read *Unfinished* chapter 3 (pp. 31–40).

In your own words answer the question, "Why did Jesus leave?"

"Whether we acknowledge it or not, every one of us has a worldview, and it influences almost every dimension of our lives: our attitudes, our values, our decisions, and our behavior. It influences that way we relate to our neighbors, our communities, and even other nations. It influences our education, our career choices, and the way we use our money. Perhaps most importantly, our worldview even influences the way we understand our faith."   *(p. 39)*

How does your background impact your worldview?

How does your worldview impact your faith in a positive way?

How might it influence your faith in a negative way?

> "As followers of Christ, we should want to embrace his view of the world. We should want to see the world as he must see it, love the world as he loves it, and live in the world as he would want us to live. We should weep for what he weeps for and treasure what he treasures." *(p. 40)*

What is Christ's view of the world?

What do you think God weeps for?

What do you think God treasures?

CHAPTER 4: MAGIC KINGDOM, TRAGIC KINGDOM, AND THE KINGDOM OF GOD?

Read *Unfinished* chapter 4 (pp. 41–54).

Describe your experience of reading chapter 4 in three words.

> "Any wealthy country can easily produce what I call Magic Kingdom Christians—Christians who have been sheltered and shaped by their affluent culture.... Most Magic Kingdom Christians don't know much about the Tragic Kingdom; in fact, they go out of their way to avoid it."
>
> *(pp. 46, 50)*

On a scale of 1 to 10 (with 1 being "not at all" and 10 being "afraid so"), rate the degree to which you may be a Magic Kingdom Christian; then explain your rating.

If you live in the Magic Kingdom, is that all bad?

Do you agree with Rich that most Magic Kingdom Christians avoid the Tragic Kingdom? Why or why not?

> "Christ did not call us to retreat from the world's pain but to enter it. He called us to go." *(p. 54)*

What does it mean to enter the world's pain?

Do you know anyone who does this well?

Where are you being called to enter the world's pain? What will make this hard or easy?

CHAPTER 5: THE MISSION OF GOD

Read *Unfinished* chapter 5 (pp. 55–66).

> "We have misunderstood the gospel to be simply the good news that our sins can be forgiven and that we can enter eternal life by believing in Jesus Christ, period. And while this is an important element of the gospel, it is not the whole gospel." *(p. 57)*

Did you resonate with Rich's claim that he had not learned the whole gospel?

What is the "whole" gospel?

"I had embraced the call to make a *decision* for Christ rather
than the call to become a *disciple* of Christ ... the good news
of the gospel [then] is not that I can enter God's kingdom
when I die; it is that Christ's death and resurrection opens
the kingdom of God to me *now*."   *(pp. 60–61)*

In your own words, what is the connection between faith and action?

In your faith story, were you taught to be more of a decider or a disciple?

What does it mean to you to be part of God's kingdom *now*?

GROUP STUDY

INTRODUCTION

The group time in session one closed with the best-known prayer in the New Testament: the Lord's Prayer. This is a prayer that Jesus taught to his disciples when they asked him how they should pray— and it marked them as his followers. After addressing God as Father and declaring God's holiness, the very first petition in the prayer is that God's will be done and his kingdom come "on earth as it is in heaven." On earth as it is in heaven? What could this mean? For many Christians, heaven is about what happens after we die and the earth is where we live in the meantime. Jesus, it seems, had another idea.

God's kingdom is the place where things are as God wants them to be. It is the dimension of reality where God runs the show and his rule and reign are implemented. In the Lord's Prayer, Jesus seems to expect that this rule and reign will happen on the earth in the present time. He longs for the ways of heaven to be a reality in the *here and now*, not just something Christians wait for *then and there*.

In chapter 1 of *Unfinished*, Rich suggested that there are three choices people make "when confronted with the incredible mystery of our existence: believe there is no story, make up your own story, or become part of God's story" (p. 22). His contention is that we find our true purpose and calling when we discover the unique part we were created to play in God's grand narrative. Which leads to an obvious question: What is that story exactly?

Starting with creation and moving through Abraham, Israel, and exile, Rich explains that God's big story is first and foremost a love story. It is a love story about a Father reaching out to his children and pursuing their redemption for the sake of redeeming the whole world. God's desire is that things here on earth would be as he has always desired them to be, and when Jesus shows up, he declares that the time for this to happen is now! Jesus announces that the kingdom of God is "at hand," and through his ministry, death on the cross, and bodily resurrection, he accomplishes this amazing feat. Then, just as God's new creation is bursting forth in the midst of our old one, Jesus does something most unexpected: he leaves.

That is where we pick up this week.

Why did Jesus leave? And if God's kingdom has come on earth as it is in heaven, then why are things still so broken in our world? And if things are still so broken, what is the role of Jesus' followers (the church) in doing something about it? These are the questions that drive session two and call us to reflect on how the Christian faith is as much about our life now as it is about an afterlife later.

CHECKING IN

The personal section of "Doing the Word" last week invited you to perform a thankless act of kindness.

What did you do? Did you learn anything from the experience that you would like to share?

HEARING THE WORD

Read Matthew 25:31–45 out loud twice in the group. If possible, use two different readers. Then answer the questions that follow.

> "When the Son of Man comes in his glory, and all the angels with him, he will sit on his glorious throne. All the nations will be gathered before him, and he will separate the people one from another as a shepherd separates the sheep from the goats. He will put the sheep on his right and the goats on his left.
>
> "Then the King will say to those on his right, 'Come, you who are blessed by my Father; take your inheritance, the kingdom prepared for you since the creation of the world.

For I was hungry and you gave me something to eat, I was thirsty and you gave me something to drink, I was a stranger and you invited me in, I needed clothes and you clothed me, I was sick and you looked after me, I was in prison and you came to visit me.'

"Then the righteous will answer him, 'Lord, when did we see you hungry and feed you, or thirsty and give you something to drink? When did we see you a stranger and invite you in, or needing clothes and clothe you? When did we see you sick or in prison and go to visit you?'

"The King will reply, 'Truly I tell you, whatever you did for one of the least of these brothers and sisters of mine, you did for me.'

"Then he will say to those on his left, 'Depart from me, you who are cursed, into the eternal fire prepared for the devil and his angels. For I was hungry and you gave me nothing to eat, I was thirsty and you gave me nothing to drink, I was a stranger and you did not invite me in, I needed clothes and you did not clothe me, I was sick and in prison and you did not look after me.'

"They also will answer, 'Lord, when did we see you hungry or thirsty or a stranger or needing clothes or sick or in prison, and did not help you?'

"He will reply, 'Truly I tell you, whatever you did not do for one of the least of these, you did not do for me.'"

What is the connection here between God and people who are poor, in need, or vulnerable?

When you hear this teaching of Jesus, does it sound like good news? Why or why not?

WATCH THE VIDEO

Watch the session two video clip, using the space below to take notes. When the video ends, take a moment to jot down one or two things that you learned, disagreed with, or were surprised by.

VIDEO DISCUSSION

First Impressions

1. Turn to one or two people next to you and finish this sentence: "After watching the video clip, one question I now, have is ..."

Community Reflection

2. Rich says we live in a world where "some have it better than others." Where have you seen this disparity? Why do you think this is the way the world is?

3. According to Rich, what is the difference between the Magic Kingdom and the Tragic Kingdom? How do you think God feels about the difference? How do you feel about it? If your feelings don't match God's, why do you think that is so?

4. Is it bad or wrong for Christians to live in the Magic Kingdom or are there disadvantages?

5. How did you experience the Pattersons' story? Was their story inspiring to you or threatening? Why?

6. If there are things in your life that medicate you from seeing global needs, what are they? Are they all "bad"? What would it mean for you to give them up? Could you do it? Why or why not?

7. Rich says that before Jesus left he gave us an assignment: to work with God to bring in his kingdom. Where do you see yourself already fulfilling that assignment? Where do you want to grow?

EXPLORING THE WORD

Read the following passages of Scripture out loud as a group, and then answer the related questions.

"And this gospel of the kingdom will be preached in the whole world as a testimony to all nations, and then the end will come." *(Matthew 24:14)*

Then Jesus came to them and said, "All authority in heaven and on earth has been given to me. Therefore go and make disciples of all nations, baptizing them in the name of the Father and of the Son and of the Holy Spirit, and teaching them to obey everything I have commanded you. And surely I am with you always, to the very end of the age." *(Matthew 28:18–20)*

What is the "gospel of the kingdom" and how does preaching it require more than words?

43

What is the difference between making a disciple and making a convert?

How do these two Scriptures connect with Matthew 25:31–45, which we read earlier?

DOING THE WORD

During the video, Rich shares some staggering statistics about hunger, need, and human suffering in the world. This week you are invited to act on that data!

As a group, consider what you already have that you can leverage to lessen suffering in the world. These assets can be time, talent, influence, and/or treasure. Conspire as a group to answer the following questions:

What needs do we feel called to meet? (Consider what things you heard in the video that stirred you, or any passions you bring with you.)

What organizations can we support that are already working to help these areas? (This is a helpful place to start this exercise, because the point is to act immediately and decisively, not do something elaborate such as begin a new nonprofit organization.)

What resources does our group have that we can offer this organization? (Again, consider time, talent, influence, and treasure.)

Is there anything you are called to sell so that you may give more generously? (Follow the Pattersons' example from the video. They took the challenge from *The Hole in Our Gospel* and asked God, "What is in our hands?" What they found were a mortgage and a sprinkler system, which they used to help bring in God's kingdom. What is in your hands?)

What would be the wrong way to undertake an exercise like this?

Now, make your plan and commit to accomplish it this week. Remember, your efforts do not have to be Herculean, just faithful. The purpose of this exercise is to activate Christian discipleship in a real yet measured way.

CLOSING PRAYER

Close the meeting again with the version of the Lord's Prayer you prayed in session one:

> Our Father in heaven, hallowed be your name,
> your kingdom come, your will be done,
>> on earth as it is in heaven.
> Give us today our daily bread.
> Forgive us our sins
>> as we forgive those who sin against us.
> Save us from the time of trial,
>> and deliver us from evil.
> For the kingdom, the power, and the glory are yours,
>> now and forever. Amen.

PERSONAL ACTIVITY

LIVING THE WORD

In *Unfinished*, Rich says that, "Christ did not call us to retreat from the world's pain but to enter it" (p. 54). This week's "Living the Word" involves taking a small step into the pain of the world.

You are invited to fast from something for twenty-four hours as an act of solidarity with people who are poor, in need, and vulnerable. This can be food (make sure you drink water), coffee, sugar, music, media devices of any kind, etc. The point is to create a scenario where you experience discomfort and give up something you feel like you need. Then, every time a hunger pain or craving comes over you, take it as an opportunity to pray. Pray for people who go without every day. Pray for God to move the church to meet the needs of the world in Jesus' name. Pray that this exercise will give you courage to "enter the world's pain" wherever you encounter it.

Write about your experience below so that you can briefly share about it during the check-in portion of session three.

What did you choose to do?

What was your experience like?

THE INVITATION
OF GOD

"God wants to use you and he wants to use me to change the world."

(Unfinished video)

Based on chapters 6–8 of the Unfinished *book*

CHAPTER 6: THE INVITATION OF GOD

Read *Unfinished* chapter 6 (pp. 67–81).

> "Tragically, many Christians make the decision (for Christ), get their certificate, but never really move in to become full citizens of God's kingdom."   *(p. 68)*

Did you resonate with Rich's observation about many Christians not becoming full citizens of God's kingdom? Why or why not?

What, in your opinion, does it mean to become a "full" citizen of the kingdom of God?

> "God's deepest desire is not that we would help the poor ... God's deepest desire is that we would love the poor; for if we love them, we will surely help them."   *(p. 76)*

Reflect on this quote for a moment. Is there a difference between helping someone and loving them?

Why does God want both?

> "The revolutionary power of the gospel is rooted in the fact that it is good news for every dimension of human life. It is not simply a system of beliefs for us to study and then proclaim; it is a different way of living we are called to adopt and demonstrate." *(pp. 80–81)*

When you read that the gospel is good news for "every dimension of human life," does that sound like good news to you? Why or why not?

What dimensions of your life, if any, do you keep from the influence of the gospel?

What is the proper connection between belief and action in the Christian faith?

CHAPTER 7: RSVP

Read *Unfinished* chapter 7 (pp. 83–92).

> "What is the most valuable thing you possess? Would you be willing to offer it to Jesus?"
> *(p. 86)*

Does this question feel more like an invitation of freedom to you or more like a threat? Explain.

Take a moment to truly reflect on Rich's question. Now answer it. Will you really lay down the most valuable things in your life at the feet of Jesus?

> "After saying yes to God, I experienced the privilege of serving on the front lines of the kingdom, the satisfaction of joining God's great mission, the wonder of discovering gifts and talents I had never before used, and the joy of feeling for the first time in my life that I was doing what I was created to do." *(p. 91)*

Rich uses this quote to describe his experience of moving from the private sector to becoming president of World Vision. What do you feel *you* were created to do?

Where do you see the needs of the world intersecting with the gifts and talents God has given you?

If you want to act, pray right now that God would bring these two things (your talents and the world's needs) together. Record your prayer below.

CHAPTER 8: LET'S MAKE A DEAL

Read *Unfinished* chapter 8 (pp. 93–102).

> "What are you clinging to? There are so many things that compete with God in our lives." *(p. 95)*

One of the questions for chapter 7 asked you to consider what it would mean to lay down the most valuable things in your life at the feet of Jesus. Picking up on the story of the rich young ruler, Rich revisits the idea here by asking, "What are you clinging to?" How do you answer that question?

Why do you cling to the things that you do?

What do the things you cling to say about your heart's desires?

> "God was showing me with great finality that I should rely
> only on him alone for my security."   *(p. 98)*

Where does your sense of safety come from?

Why is it hard to trust God for our security?

What are the implications for communities, cities, and even nations to trust God alone for their security? What are these entities tempted to trust instead? What are you tempted to trust instead?

GROUP STUDY

INTRODUCTION

Philosophers are in the business of describing reality—no easy feat. Each era of human history has its own set of assumptions, blind spots, and wisdom about "the way things really are," and this keeps philosophers on their toes. They consistently face new challenges in creating the categories and distinctions that help people make sense of the world they live in.

Now, whether or not philosophy is your thing, most people can appreciate the contribution of one of the twentieth century's most well-known philosophers, Jean Baudrillard. Baudrillard was a French philosopher who proposed that the way many in our world experience reality is through something called *simulacra* (from the word "simulation"). *Simulacra* is the imitation of something real that, over time, becomes accepted as the real thing itself; for example, when someone thinks that Cool-Whip is real whipped cream or that the country of Morocco in Walt Disney World's Epcot Center is the same thing as the actual Morocco.

Rich makes the point that most Christians in affluent societies live in a *simulacra* version of the world—what he calls the Magic Kingdom. In the Magic Kingdom, the world's problems are reduced to such things as choices about vacations, decorating, and keeping up with the Joneses; the world's real problems are best left unknown or avoided altogether. Because of our life in the Magic Kingdom, we have become a church blinded to the sphere in which much of the world lives—what Rich calls the Tragic Kingdom. This kingdom is characterized by hunger, fear, injustice, and oppression because the basic needs of human life are either in short supply or outright withheld.

Many say the disparity between the Magic Kingdom and Tragic Kingdom can only be reconciled by an act of God. But that's good news because, in Christ, we believe that God has already acted—decisively. Jesus' death on the cross has ushered in a new reality, the kingdom of God. In the kingdom of God, things are as God wants them to be but with one big caveat: God will not grow his kingdom alone. He wants to do it with us.

In the story of Jesus' glorious ascension, we find a God who has longed to work with people to further the creation since Genesis 1, turning the whole enterprise over to his precious children to accomplish its renewal. This is why Jesus left. It was not the Father's will for him to renew all things by himself. God wants to do it with us—and now, thanks to his Spirit, we are actually equipped for the job.

All of this sets up session three. If Jesus turned over his kingdom's accomplishment to us, what if we don't take him up on his invitation? Or—and maybe this is more threatening—what if we *do* take him up on his invitation? What will it mean for us to RSVP "yes" to God's invitation? What will we be asked to bring to the party?

CHECKING IN

Reflect on the two challenges that came out of session two. One was to act as a group to meet a real need in the world; the other was to take on an ascetic practice to demonstrate solidarity with and better pray for the poor.

What did you do and why? What did you learn about yourself? What did you learn about God?

HEARING THE WORD

Read Matthew 22:1–14 out loud twice in the group. If possible, use two different readers. Then answer the questions that follow.

> Jesus spoke to them again in parables, saying: "The kingdom of heaven is like a king who prepared a wedding banquet for his son. He sent his servants to those who had been invited to the banquet to tell them to come, but they refused to come.

"Then he sent some more servants and said, 'Tell those who have been invited that I have prepared my dinner: My oxen and fattened cattle have been butchered, and everything is ready. Come to the wedding banquet.'

"But they paid no attention and went off—one to his field, another to his business. The rest seized his servants, mistreated them and killed them. The king was enraged. He sent his army and destroyed those murderers and burned their city.

"Then he said to his servants, 'The wedding banquet is ready, but those I invited did not deserve to come. So go to the street corners and invite to the banquet anyone you find.' So the servants went out into the streets and gathered all the people they could find, the bad as well as the good, and the wedding hall was filled with guests.

"But when the king came in to see the guests, he noticed a man there who was not wearing wedding clothes. He asked, 'How did you get in here without wedding clothes, friend?' The man was speechless.

"Then the king told the attendants, 'Tie him hand and foot, and throw him outside, into the darkness, where there will be weeping and gnashing of teeth.'

"For many are invited, but few are chosen."

Why do the invitees reject the king's invitation? What are some of the reasons people reject God's invitation today?

Why do you think Jesus tells this parable?

WATCH THE VIDEO

Watch the session three video clip, using the space below to take notes. When the video ends, take a moment to jot down one or two things that you learned, disagreed with, or were surprised by.

VIDEO DISCUSSION

First Impressions

1. Turn to one or two people next to you and finish this sentence: "After watching the video clip, one question I now have is ..."

Community Reflection

2. Rich says that we are invited to join God in changing the world. On a scale of 1 to 10 (with 10 being "exciting" and 1 being "exhausting"), rate how this invitation feels to you today. Why did you answer as you did?

3. Is it ever too late to RSVP to God's invitation? Why or why not?

4. What did you think about Margo's story? What prompted her to accept God's invitation in a fresh way? How does her story challenge you?

5. In her testimony, Margo says, "My life has become ten times richer than I ever dreamed it could be—not because I've held the things that I have closer to myself, but because I've given them and given them willingly." What is the connection between joy and generosity? Does one always follow the other? Why or why not?

6. Rich outlines three steps in saying yes to the invitation to follow Jesus' Great Commission. They are: (1) submit to God's rule in our lives; (2) join communities that share God's values; and (3) go into the world as God's ambassadors. Which of these three comes easy for you? Which one is the most difficult? What can you do this week to strengthen your areas of weakness?

7. Rich asks the question: "What would love do?" Do you know people who make choices like this in their lives? What are they like? Do you make choices in your life based on love? Why or why not?

EXPLORING THE WORD

Read the following passages of Scripture out loud as a group, and then answer the related questions.

> "You are the salt of the earth. But if the salt loses its saltiness, how can it be made salty again? It is no longer good for anything, except to be thrown out and trampled underfoot." *(Matthew 5:13)*

> Therefore, if anyone is in Christ, the new creation has come: The old has gone, the new is here! All this is from God, who reconciled us to himself through Christ and gave us

the ministry of reconciliation: that God was reconciling the world to himself in Christ, not counting people's sins against them. And he has committed to us the message of reconciliation. We are therefore Christ's ambassadors, as though God were making his appeal through us. We implore you on Christ's behalf: Be reconciled to God. God made him who had no sin to be sin for us, so that in him we might become the righteousness of God.   *(2 Corinthians 5:17–21)*

Salt is a preservative and a spice. How do each of these facts relate to Jesus' call for us to be salt in the world?

In 2 Corinthians 5:20 the church in Corinth is reminded that they are "Christ's ambassadors" and that "God [is] making his appeal through [them]." What "appeal" is God making?

DOING THE WORD/CLOSING PRAYER

In the video this week, Rich suggests that the best way to make our choices according God's way in the world is to ask the question, "What would love do?" This week your group will put this practice into action.

Generate a list of three authentic moral questions, cares, and concerns the group has brought with them to the study. These can be anything from personal problems in the community to global issues.

Once the list is generated, spend a few minutes praying as a group and exploring the question, "What would love do?" for each of the items listed. Then seek to generate at least one concrete action of love that your group can accomplish for each item.

Finally, adopt one of the actions listed to perform during the coming week. Some may be too specific for more than one person and that's okay. There will be others that can accommodate several folks (the more people who pray for something, the better). Take notes on your experience and bring them to share during check-in next week.

PERSONAL ACTIVITY

LIVING THE WORD

During session three, your *Unfinished* study group took stock of the real needs of their community and resolved to act on them in the name of Jesus. Your "Living the Word" time for this session involves keeping that promise.

What need did you commit to act upon, meet, or pray for? During the coming week, remember what you committed to and make good on that pledge. If you were not present for the last session, consider the needs (large and small) in your community today. What is one thing you can do (sharing resources, giving money, offering words of encouragement, praying, etc.) to meet one of those needs today? Once you have identified the need, move to act in Jesus' name. Promise-keeping is part of the character of God. Make it part of your character as well.

Write about your experience below.

WE WERE
MADE FOR MORE

"It's not your career; it's not your family; it's not your abilities, gifts, skills and talents, or money and possessions that bring meaning and purpose to your life. Rather it's the purpose of your life that brings meaning to everything else."

(*Unfinished* video)

PRE-SESSION PERSONAL STUDY

Based on chapters 9–11 of the Unfinished *book*

CHAPTER 9: WE WERE MADE FOR MORE

Read *Unfinished* chapter 6 (pp. 103–115).

"How do you see your life?" *(p. 103)*

Do you ever feel like you are just "going through the motions" in your life? If not, why? If so, when do you most feel that way?

Do you enjoy your life? Why or why not?

Rich says that many people's life goals are to be successful, comfortable, wealthy, famous, and happy (pp. 107–108). Answering honestly, are any of these your life goals too?

If so, which one is most tempting to you and why? If not, what *is* your life goal?

> "All work is sacred if it does not violate God's laws and if it is offered in the service of building his kingdom. When we speak of God's calling on our lives, it is a calling away from our own agendas, a leaving behind of our hopes and dreams to embrace his hopes and dreams for our lives."
>
> *(pp. 111–112)*

What is a hope or dream for your life that would be hard to leave behind?

What is one practical way that what you do for a living (or how you live as a retiree or student) can build God's kingdom?

CHAPTER 10: GOD'S SPIRITUAL GPS

Read *Unfinished* chapter 10 (pp. 117–127).

> "For most of us, the Holy Spirit is one of the great mysteries of our faith. I truly believe it is impossible for us to fully comprehend the profound significance of God literally dwelling within us in the manifestation of his Holy Spirit."
>
> *(p. 118)*

How much do you think about the Holy Spirit?

Is the Holy Spirit important to the way you practice your Christianity? Why did you answer as you did?

> "[The Holy Spirit] is nothing less than the single enabling power that now makes it possible for ordinary human beings to be transformed and live differently than was ever before possible."
>
> *(p. 121)*

On pages 121–122, Rich lists thirteen different gifts, powers, and abilities that the Holy Spirit gives every Christian for life and ministry. Look over the list. Which of these "powers" do you desire most? Why?

Which gifts do you already see at work in your life? Where have you seen them?

CHAPTER 11: CALLED FOR A PURPOSE

Read *Unfinished* chapter 11 (pp. 129–143).

> "I do think that there are some helpful and logical steps, derived from Scripture, that can bring greater clarity to this universal longing to know God's will for our lives. Let me suggest six of them: Commit, Pray, Prepare, Obey, Act, Trust." *(p. 131)*

After reading Rich's description of each step, consider: Which of the six come naturally to you? Which are the most difficult?

Are you following God's call for your life?

GROUP STUDY

INTRODUCTION

J. R. R. Tolkien's Lord of the Rings books are among the most popular of all time. The fact that the trilogy (and its precursor, *The Hobbit*) have sold hundreds of millions of copies speaks not only to the intrigue of the stories but also to the resonance readers feel with the title character, Frodo Baggins. When we first meet Frodo, he is an unremarkable thirty-three-year-old hobbit overshadowed by his much more famous uncle Bilbo.

But when Bilbo gives his nephew a magic ring that makes its wearer invisible, Frodo's ho-hum life begins to change—especially when the wizard Gandalf determines the ring to be the One Ring forged by the Dark Lord thousands of years earlier that would enable him to enslave all of Middle-earth. Faced with the task of destroying the ring to break its curse, Frodo accepts the challenge and in the process discovers that his life has a much bigger, grander, and more important meaning than he ever thought possible. He is to be instrumental in the defeat of evil in his world.

One of the reasons readers love Frodo so much is that they, like him, long to find their purpose. The fantastic world of Middle-earth serves as a backdrop for a story about an "average guy" embracing what he was born to do. This is what all of us want. We want to know what we were born to do and we want that "something" to be important.

If you resonate with this yearning, then there is good news for you! You too were born to do something meaningful with your life! Your calling is important! And, what's best, this purpose and calling is something you can actually discover! However, like Frodo Baggins, it all starts by accepting an invitation.

God has given an invitation to all of us. It is an invitation to find our life's purpose by joining his mission in the world. However, we each have to accept the offer. We have to, as Rich says, RSVP to the party. And once we say yes, the question still remains: How do we actually get where we've said we are willing to go? Once we have committed to the journey, where do we go next? These are the questions that drive session four. How do we find our meaning and purpose in God's kingdom, and what will it take to embrace it?

CHECKING IN

Last week your group took stock of the needs of your community and the world and asked the question, "What would love do?" This generated some concrete actions, one of which each group member was invited to adopt.

If you've fulfilled this assignment, share what your experience was like by addressing the following questions:

Was this a difficult or easy task to integrate into your normal life? Did you learn anything about yourself through this process? Did you learn anything about God?

HEARING THE WORD

Read Matthew 16:24–27 out loud twice in the group. If possible, use two different readers. Then answer the questions that follow.

> Then Jesus said to his disciples, "Whoever wants to be my disciple must deny themselves and take up their cross and follow me. For whoever wants to save their life will lose it, but whoever loses their life for me will find it. What good will it be for someone to gain the whole world, yet forfeit their soul? Or what can anyone give in exchange for their

71

soul? For the Son of Man is going to come in his Father's glory with his angels, and then he will reward each person according to what they have done."

Think of someone you know who has "taken up their cross." What did that look like in this person's life?

What is the connection between discipleship and suffering?

WATCH THE VIDEO

Watch the session four video clip, using the space below to take notes. When the video ends, take a moment to jot down one or two things that you learned, disagreed with, or were surprised by.

VIDEO DISCUSSION

First Impressions

1. Turn to one or two people next to you and finish this sentence: "After watching the video clip, one question I want to ask is ..."

Community Reflection

2. Rich opens the video by saying that our lives can sometimes fall into a rut without our realizing it. Have you ever felt like your life was in a rut? Why or why not? Do you experience your life as being more one of fulfillment or more one of "quiet desperation"? Explain.

3. What makes you want to get out of bed in the morning? Or, put another way, what are you passionate about? The examples from the video involve job and career, but does our passion have to rest there? What else can give our lives purpose and meaning?

4. On a scale of 1 to 10 (1 being "closed" and 10 being "very open"), how open are you to God's will for your life? What made you answer as you did?

5. Both Rich and Jim talk about how their work got in the way of following God's will. What are other things that get in the way of being open to God's will? What gets in the way of *you* being open to God's will? What can you do about that?

6. In the video, Jim mentions that when he realized God was right beside him everywhere he went, it was a game changer. How do you think about the presence of God? Is God close or far off? How does your view of where God is shape your faith, and is this a positive or negative thing?

7. Rich says, "It's not your career; it's not your family; it's not your abilities, gifts, skills and talents, or money and possessions that bring meaning and purpose to your life. Rather it's the *purpose* of your life

that brings meaning to everything else." Do you agree with Rich? If not, why? If so, are you living this way? What makes living this way difficult?

EXPLORING THE WORD

Read the following Scripture out loud as a group, and then answer the related questions.

> "Anyone who loves their father or mother more than me is not worthy of me; anyone who loves their son or daughter more than me is not worthy of me. Whoever does not take up their cross and follow me is not worthy of me. Whoever finds their life will lose it, and whoever loses their life for my sake will find it." *(Matthew 10:37–39)*

What is Jesus getting at with this teaching? Does it feel like he's being extreme?

Do you feel that you are worthy of Jesus and taking up your cross to follow him? Why or why not?

75

DOING THE WORD/CLOSING PRAYER

Your "Doing the Word" group time for this session involves an ancient Christian discipline known as "practicing the presence of God."

As Jim mentioned in the video, becoming aware of the nearness of God in his daily life radically shifted his perspective and priorities. Christians over the centuries have come to the same conclusion, and so the great contemplative traditions of the church developed. You get to take part in one of them right now.

As a group, sit in a comfortable position, close your eyes, and begin to breathe slowly. A designated group leader will remind everyone that Jesus is with the group even now; God is indeed in this place. Then the group leader will invite group members to silently repeat the phrase, "God, you are here." Next, the group leader will invite group members to silently repeat the phrase, "God, I am here." Repeat this two-phrase prayer for five minutes, with the group leader alone keeping time. It's okay if you get distracted; just keep coming back to your prayer.

Conclude the time by praying the Lord's Prayer together (see session one or session two).

Then briefly respond to these questions:

Did you feel as if God was near? Why or why not?

What worked for you in this experience? What didn't work for you?

PERSONAL ACTIVITY

LIVING THE WORD

Revisit "practicing the presence of God" this week by finding five to ten minutes in your schedule to be present to God without talking. It can be during your drive to work (with no radio, of course). It can be a walk during your lunch break. It can be in a church, in your home, or outside. The only stipulation is that you intentionally spend the time being as present to the Creator as you are able to be. Use the prayer from the group time if that is helpful. When you are done, answer the following question in preparation for the check-in portion of session five.

How would you describe your experience using only three words?

SPIRITUAL DOMINOES

"God had chosen a different way, a new way, to change the world. He had chosen the weak over the powerful, the humble over the noble, the poor over the rich, the servant over the master; he had chosen a baby in a manger over a king in a palace."

(*Unfinished*, p. 153)

PRE-SESSION PERSONAL STUDY

Based on chapters 12–13 of the Unfinished *book*

CHAPTER 12: SPIRITUAL DOMINOES

Read *Unfinished* chapter 12 (pp. 145–160).

> "This is exactly how God works in history. Most of the stories in the Bible illustrate the incredible impact of ordinary people willing to be used by God, setting off a chain reaction that had profound significance later." *(p. 146)*

When you think of times when God acted in history, which stories do you first think of?

Based on how you answered, consider: Do the stories you recalled involve spectacular activity by God or ordinary activity by God? Is God working alone in the stories or with someone else?

Is there a difference in how God works today?

Does anything about your answer disclose your true thoughts about how God works in the world?

> "The apostle Paul understood that the Christian movement in the first century had to be carried by ordinary people. From a worldly perspective, early Christianity was hanging by a thread, led by a rough band of men described in the book of Acts as unschooled and ordinary." *(p. 153)*

Why do you think God did not use the wealthy, well-heeled, powerful, and famous people of the first century to change the world?

SPIRITUAL DOMINOES

Does God work the same way today?

What *is* the role of wealth, celebrity, and power in God's spiritual dominoes?

> "Have you given up? Have you concluded that the cards you've been dealt are not a winning hand? Have you convinced yourself that God can't use someone like you — that you're a loser? Are you, maybe, even angry with God for dealing you those cards in the first place? Are you tired of picking yourself up after every failure and setback? *(p. 159)*

Rich tells the story of Abraham Lincoln and then follows up with the set of questions in the above quote. How would you answer these questions?

Do you feel like God dealt you a "bad hand" in life?

Do you see your story more as one of victimization or victory?

How does God see your story? Is there a difference between your version and God's?

CHAPTER 13: OUTPOSTS OF THE KINGDOM

Read *Unfinished* chapter 13 (pp. 161–180).

> "The big story of God is not yet finished. The next chapter
> is being written by the church."   *(p. 164)*

What is the first thing that comes to mind when you hear the word "church"?

Are your associations with church positive or negative? Explain.

What is your working definition of "church"?

> "It is as if we have been vaccinated by a weaker strain of
> Jesus that makes us resistant to the real thing. I pray for a
> strain for which there is no vaccine." *(p. 169)*

Do you agree with this diagnosis of Christianity in your country? Why or why not?

What would a "strain for which there is no vaccine" look like?

Rich identifies five traps that churches can fall into that keep them from realizing their full potential as change agents for God's kingdom. They are (1) valuing belief over behavior, (2) replacing exhortation with explanation, (3) turning inward instead of outward, (4) allowing apathy to replace outrage, and (5) prioritizing institution over revolution. Reread pages 170–175 and consider:

Which trap seems the most dangerous to you?

Which of these traps are you most likely to fall into and why?

How do you go about getting out of one (or more) of these traps once you're in them?

GROUP STUDY

INTRODUCTION

Science fiction plots involving time travel often employ something called "the butterfly effect." Derived from chaos theory in mathematics, the butterfly effect suggests that small, seemingly insignificant actions in one part of a system can lead to massive consequences in another. It got its name because, it is said, something as simple as a butterfly flapping its wings today can create conditions that swirl together to cause a hurricane down the road. This week in *Unfinished*, we are asked to consider if, in God's economy, this is actually true.

Using the example of dominoes, Rich challenges us to consider the significance of small actions in our lives. Because God is moving to heal and restore the whole creation, even small acts of faith, hope, and love can contribute to the incredible change God is bringing about. Moreover, as much as all of us have a part to play in God's great story, we must not think we are in it alone. We are part of a team, and that team is called the church. God plans to use the gifts and talents of his *whole* church to keep nudging creation toward its eventual renewal, not just a few "holy people."

In John's gospel, Jesus tells his disciples two remarkable things. First, he gives them a new commandment, telling them that they are to "love one another as I have loved you" (John 13:34). Second, he explains that the disciples' love and unity would let the world know that he has been truly sent by God. Think about that. The church proclaims that Jesus is king not through our perfect doctrine, vocal advocacy on social issues, or even acts of service. No, the good news of God's rescue is most loudly proclaimed by the church's love and unity (John 17:22–23).

Love and unity. These two items are central to Jesus' instruction, and yet neither can be accomplished alone. We need each other to finish the job Jesus has entrusted to us, and that is where session five picks up. Does God really work through small actions to effect change? And if so, how are his communities (the church) supposed to implement that work together?

CHECKING IN

Last week you were invited to "practice the presence of God" as a group and on your own. Debrief the experience:

Did you find this practice easy or difficult? Was it tedious or life-giving? Does silence and contemplation come naturally to you?

HEARING THE WORD

Read John 6:1–13 out loud in the group. Then answer the questions that follow.

> Some time after this, Jesus crossed to the far shore of the Sea of Galilee (that is, the Sea of Tiberias), and a great crowd of people followed him because they saw the signs he had performed by healing the sick. Then Jesus went up on a mountainside and sat down with his disciples. The Jewish Passover Festival was near.
>
> When Jesus looked up and saw a great crowd coming toward him, he said to Philip, "Where shall we buy bread for these people to eat?" He asked this only to test him, for he already had in mind what he was going to do.
>
> Philip answered him, "It would take more than half a year's wages to buy enough bread for each one to have a bite!"
>
> Another of his disciples, Andrew, Simon Peter's brother, spoke up, "Here is a boy with five small barley loaves and two small fish, but how far will they go among so many?"
>
> Jesus said, "Have the people sit down." There was plenty of grass in that place, and they sat down (about five thousand men were there). Jesus then took the loaves, gave thanks, and distributed to those who were seated as much as they wanted. He did the same with the fish.
>
> When they had all had enough to eat, he said to his

disciples, "Gather the pieces that are left over. Let nothing be wasted." So they gathered them and filled twelve baskets with the pieces of the five barley loaves left over by those who had eaten.

In this story Jesus sees a world where there is always enough. How do you see the world? Is there enough for everyone's needs? If not, why? If so, then why are there still so many needs?

What can we learn about our part in God's plan through the actions of the disciples in this story?

WATCH THE VIDEO

Watch the session five video clip, using the space below to take notes. When the video ends, take a moment to jot down one or two things that you learned, disagreed with, or were surprised by.

VIDEO DISCUSSION

First Impressions

1. Turn to one or two people next to you and finish this sentence: "After watching the video clip, one question I want to ask is ..."

Community Reflection

2. On a scale of 1 to 10 (with 1 being "not at all" and 10 being "anything is possible!"), how much do you believe that you can change the world?

3. What is the difference between changing the world and changing the world "in Jesus' name"?

4. Rich says he hears one of two things when he challenges people to join God in changing the world. First, he hears people lament that they are not rich enough, smart enough, famous enough, etc., to really make a difference; and second, he hears people say that changing the world is somebody else's job. Which of these sounds most like something you would say? Why? What would it take to change your mind?

5. Do you think God can really use ordinary things to produce the extraordinary? Why or why not?

6. What did you think about Steve Reynolds's story from the video? What needs has God put right in front of you that you can already act on in little ways? What will it mean for you to lay your life at the feet of Jesus (as the little boy lays fish and bread before him)?

7. Rich works hard this session to convince you to "think again" about the part you can play in changing the world. Does he succeed? Why or why not? What hopes or doubts will you carry with you out of this session?

EXPLORING THE WORD

Read the following Scripture out loud as a group, and then answer the related questions.

> [Jesus] told them another parable: "The kingdom of heaven is like a mustard seed, which a man took and planted in his field. Though it is the smallest of all seeds, yet when it grows, it is the largest of garden plants and becomes a tree, so that the birds come and perch in its branches."
>
> He told them still another parable: "The kingdom of heaven is like yeast that a woman took and mixed into about sixty pounds of flour until it worked all through the dough."
>
> *(Matthew 13:31–33)*

If you were asked to explain the meaning of these parables to a ten-year-old, how would you do it? What contemporary images might you use?

If Jesus says his kingdom grows in hidden, small, and unseen ways, why do we tend to feel that if our efforts are not Herculean, then they are not worth anything at all?

Are there any connections you find between this teaching and the story of Jesus feeding the five thousand that we read earlier?

DOING THE WORD/CLOSING PRAYER

You will need the following supplies for this "Doing the Word" activity:

- Current newspapers or newsmagazines (enough for every 2 people in the group to share)
- Scissors (1 pair for every 3 people)
- Glue or glue sticks (1 for every 3 people)
- Index cards (4 x 6)
- Markers, pens, and/or colored pencils

God is in the business of redemption. Where there is pain, God brings joy. Where there is violence, Jesus makes peace. Where there is scarcity, Jesus creates plenty. Today you are invited to join God by seeing the world the way he does.

Before you are recent newspapers and newsmagazines.

Scan them and find stories that strike you as scary, dark, and unhopeful.

Now, as an act of prayer and a demonstration of hope, take scissors and cut out the words and images of the article, using the glue and a writing instrument to refashion them into a prayer on one of the index cards.

These requests can be prayers for hope where there is hopelessness, prayers for peace where there is fear, or prayers for light where there is darkness.

When everyone is finished, close your time together by going around the room and sharing your prayers out loud. Then listen ... it's the sound of a domino falling.

PERSONAL ACTIVITY

LIVING THE WORD

> "What should we do then?" the crowd asked. John answered, "Anyone who has two shirts should share with the one who has none, and anyone who has food should do the same." *(Luke 3:10–11)*

When asked how to prepare for the coming of the Messiah and the kingdom of God, John the Baptist instructed people to share what they had. This week you are invited to join God in the "ordinary things" by acting in a similar manner.

This exercise is called, "If You Have Two, Give One." Consider all of your possessions (particularly the ones you are tied to). Are there any that you have more than one of? If so, this week you are invited to give one away. This can be a direct gift to someone in need or it can mean selling the item in question and donating the money. Whichever you choose, remember to perform this activity as an expression of prayer and worship, and trust that God will use it in the chain reaction of redemption he is working in the world.

Write about your experience below so that you can briefly share about it during the check-in portion of session six.

GOD'S GREAT ADVENTURE FOR YOUR LIFE

"There are as many ways to join the great mission of Christ in our world as there are people."

(*Unfinished*, p. 216)

PRE-SESSION PERSONAL STUDY

Based on chapters 14–15 of the Unfinished *book*

CHAPTER 14: THE GATES OF HELL

Read *Unfinished* chapter 14 (pp. 181–198).

> "It is critical for the church to understand that it is, in fact, caught in the midst of a great cosmic struggle between God and Satan, between good and evil." *(p. 184)*

How do you conceive of the devil or Satan?

Where do you see evil masquerading as good in our world today?

Why is it critical for the church to understand that it is caught in the middle of a cosmic struggle between good and evil?

"In the *incarnation* of God in Christ, God's government in exile returned in dramatic fashion; it returned to liberate God's children and directly challenge the dominion of Satan and sin. And in the *death and resurrection* of Christ, Satan was decisively defeated as Jesus removed the barrier of sin and alienation by paying its full price, thereby flinging wide open the doors to God's kingdom under God's reign."　*(p. 186)*

If evil is defeated on the cross, why do bad things continue to happen?

Do you have a different answer to this question after reading this chapter than you did before? Explain.

"Nothing challenges our faith or fuels our doubts more than the presence of pain, suffering, and evil in our world. "Why," we ask, "would a loving God allow such horrors?" This nagging question, perhaps more than any other, can undermine our faith and hobble our determination to storm the gates of hell."　*(p. 187)*

Do you ever feel this way?

Is asking, "Why would a loving God allow such horrors?" really the right question? If not, then what is?

> "I wonder, too, what consequences will be felt when followers of Christ desert the front lines of his revolution to settle down in comfortable lives far from the battle." *(pp. 191–192)*

Do you believe the actions of your life have this much consequence in the battle between good and evil in our world? Why or why not?

CHAPTER 15: GOD'S GREAT ADVENTURE FOR YOUR LIFE

Read *Unfinished* chapter 15 (pp. 199–216).

> "Some of us will serve right where we are. [God] wants to use our vocations, resources, networks, and skills. He can use whatever we possess — money, assets, and time. He will even use our weaknesses and flaws, our struggles and our pain as well. If they are yielded to him, he will use them."
>
> *(p. 205)*

What do you possess that God can use to bring in his kingdom?

What weakness, flaw, struggle, or pain in you would you most like to see him transform and use to his glory?

> "Aurea has no safety net, no contingency plans, and no retirement accounts—just faith in God. The truth Steve learned from her that day was this: when God is all you have, you discover that God is all you need." *(p. 205)*

Reread Aurea's story (pp. 204–205). How would you view life if you had been dealt the cards she was?

Does your life reflect the maxim that "when God is all you have, then God is all you need"? Why or why not? If not, what is keeping you from experiencing this kind of freedom?

> "You don't get to write your own obituary, but you do get to live the life that will be written about. The question is, what will be written about you?"
>
> *(p. 214)*

Think about your life to date. What would be written about you if today was your last day?

Does reflecting on this make you think differently about how you want to live tomorrow?

GROUP STUDY

INTRODUCTION

One of the realities of modern life is that tragic things happen. Pain is inescapable for everyone. And now, thanks to the Internet and twenty-four-hour news, we are more aware of it than ever. Rich notes that the question people often ask in the face of tragedy is why a good God would allow such bad things to happen.

This question is understandable and comes from a place deep in the human heart that desperately wants to make sense of the unthinkable. But even though it is driven by a God-given desire for justice and harmony, asking "Why?" is the wrong question. Not because it is unimportant but because, ultimately, it is unanswerable. Though we don't know why God allows evil, there is one thing the Scriptures *do* make very clear. They affirm that though evil is real, God has and is definitively acting to do something about it! Rich explains that when Jesus died on the cross, it marked the definitive defeat of sin and death. On Calvary, evil loses and good wins! Period. Done deal. The job of the church is to join God in implementing what Jesus accomplished by rooting out and dismantling evil wherever in the world it still has a hold. We do not do this by aping evil's tactics of intimidation, violence, and power but through acts of love, meekness, and service.

The theological term for the problem of evil is "theodicy." *Unfinished* urges us to move from a theodicy of *explanation*, asking, "Why does evil exist?" to a theodicy of *participation*, asking, "How can we join God in doing something about it?" This is the thrust of the last session. How do we deal with the reality of the powers and principalities that we war against, and what practical steps can we take to discover God's calling for our lives?

CHECKING IN

Last week you were invited to undertake an exercise called, "If You Have Two, Give One." Take a few minutes now to debrief about it.

101

Did you complete this challenge? If not, why not? If so, what was your experience like?

HEARING THE WORD

Read Mark 10:17–31 out loud in the group. Then answer the questions that follow.

> As Jesus started on his way, a man ran up to him and fell on his knees before him. "Good teacher," he asked, "what must I do to inherit eternal life?"
>
> "Why do you call me good?" Jesus answered. "No one is good—except God alone. You know the commandments: 'You shall not murder, you shall not commit adultery, you shall not steal, you shall not give false testimony, you shall not defraud, honor your father and mother.'"
>
> "Teacher," he declared, "all these I have kept since I was a boy."
>
> Jesus looked at him and loved him. "One thing you lack," he said. "Go, sell everything you have and give to the poor, and you will have treasure in heaven. Then come, follow me."
>
> At this the man's face fell. He went away sad, because he had great wealth.
>
> Jesus looked around and said to his disciples, "How hard it is for the rich to enter the kingdom of God!"
>
> The disciples were amazed at his words. But Jesus said again, "Children, how hard it is to enter the kingdom of God! It is easier for a camel to go through the eye of a needle than for someone who is rich to enter the kingdom of God."
>
> The disciples were even more amazed, and said to each other, "Who then can be saved?"
>
> Jesus looked at them and said, "With man this is impossible, but not with God; all things are possible with God."

Then Peter spoke up, "We have left everything to follow you!"

"Truly I tell you," Jesus replied, "no one who has left home or brothers or sisters or mother or father or children or fields for me and the gospel will fail to receive a hundred times as much in this present age: homes, brothers, sisters, mothers, children and fields—along with persecutions—and in the age to come eternal life. But many who are first will be last, and the last first."

If you were the rich man and Jesus told you to sell all that you had, would you do it? Why or why not?

Why do you think Jesus includes "persecutions" in verse 30? What does persecution look like for Christians where you live? What does persecution *not* look like?

WATCH THE VIDEO

Watch the session six video clip, using the space below to take notes. When the video ends, take a moment to jot down one or two things that you learned, disagreed with, or were surprised by.

VIDEO DISCUSSION

First Impressions

1. Complete this sentence: "If I could describe my *Unfinished* experience in one word, that word would be _____."
Share as a group the word you used.

Community Reflection

In the video, Rich offers six steps to finding God's special calling in our lives. For our final "Community Reflection" time we will consider the implications of each in turn.

2. **Commit:** Rich says that the first thing we have to decide is if we are "all in" or "out" when it comes to living our lives God's way. Using a "thumb read" as a scale (with thumbs up being "all in" and thumbs down being "out"), honestly answer where you are on the commitment scale today. Why did you answer as you did? What makes commitment to Jesus challenging for you?

3. **Pray:** Rich reminds us that knowing God's will means being in constant contact with him. This is what prayer is: communicating and being present with God. What does prayer look like in your life right

now? What is working in your prayer life? What is not? What is one practical way you can grow as a person of prayer?

4. **Prepare for the Journey:** It's no good heading out on a journey if we are not prepared for the trip. The Bible, says Rich, is an invaluable roadmap for our guidance and direction. How do you engage with the Bible at this time in your life? Do you read it? If so, when? If not, why not? What would make it easier for you to engage the Bible in your devotional life? What other resources (mentors, study groups, worship, spiritual direction, etc.) can help to prepare us for the journey?

5. **Be Obedient:** Saying that you will do something and actually doing it are two different things. Rich suggests that if we practice being faithful and obedient to God in the little things, we will then be ready

when it comes time to discern the big things. What is an example of one of these "little things"? What is one "little thing" you can start being faithful in today as a way of practicing obedience?

6. Act: As Rich notes, "God can't steer a parked car." We are required to get up and get moving in our Christianity if we want to join God's mission in the world. Keeping in mind the video's example of the people of Jerusalem each rebuilding the portion of the city wall that was closest to them, (1) what is the need nearest you that you have consistently avoided, and (2) what one action can you take to be a rebuilder for God in this specific area?

7. Trust: If we are faithfully engaged in the other five steps, Rich reminds us to relax. We can trust God to work everything out according to his purpose and timing. Mother Teresa is quoted during the video as saying, "We can do no great things—only small things with great love." Is this is true? Is your life motivated by great love? Is it hard or easy for you to trust God?

EXPLORING THE WORD

Reread or reconsider the story of the rich young ruler we read earlier from Mark 10:17–31, and then answer the related questions.

Why do possessions make it hard to come to God?

Is it wrong to have possessions?

What do you think the difference is between treasure on earth and treasure in heaven?

DOING THE WORD

Writing Your Own Obituary

You will need the following supplies for this "Doing the Word" activity:

- Two pieces of paper for each participant
- Pens

Rich challenged us during the video to write our own obituary, and that is what we are going to do for our final "Doing the Word."

Using the supplies provided, on the first piece of paper write down the answer to this question: "If you were to die tonight, what would people say about you in your memorial service? How would you be remembered?" Take about five minutes to work on this.

On the other piece of paper, answer the following question, "What would you like to be remembered for?" Again, take five minutes to complete this. Now compare the two and answer this question:

What are the differences? What are the similarities? Where do you need a new beginning?

Go around the room and share your observations. Then name three concrete steps you each can take to implement what you have learned in this study. How can you be the answer to someone else's prayer?

CLOSING PRAYER

Close the session with this "Prayer of Self-Dedication" from the Book of Common Prayer:

> Almighty and eternal God, so draw our hearts to You,
> so guide our minds,
> so fill our imaginations,
> so control our wills,
> that we may be wholly Yours, utterly dedicated unto You;
> and then use us, we pray You, as You will,
> and always to Your glory
> and the welfare of Your people;
> through our Lord and Savior Jesus Christ. Amen.

Now go forth and be finishers of God's work in Jesus' name!

GROUP LEADER NOTES

THANK YOU FOR giving of your time and talent to lead an *Unfinished* group study.

The *Unfinished* experience is a six-session study built around weekly small group gatherings (or however often your group meets). As group leader, imagine yourself as the host of a dinner party whose job is manage all the behind-the-scenes details so your guests can focus on each other and interaction around the topic.

You need not answer all the questions or reteach the content—the book, video, and study guide do most of that work. This makes your small group more of a learning community—a place to process, question, and reflect on what the author, Rich Stearns, is teaching.

Make sure everyone in the group gets a copy of this study guide. Encourage them to write in their guide and bring it with them every week. This will keep everyone on the same page and help the session run more smoothly. Likewise, encourage every participant (or every couple) to get a copy of the *Unfinished* book so they can complete the pre-session personal study at the start of each session (gray background pages). If this is not possible, see if anyone from the group is willing to donate an extra copy or two for sharing. Giving everyone access to all the material will help this study be as rewarding an experience as possible.

Hospitality

As group leader, you'll want to create an environment conducive to sharing and learning. A church sanctuary or classroom may not be ideal for this kind of meeting because those venues can feel formal and less intimate. Wherever you choose, make sure there is enough comfortable seating for everyone and, if possible, arrange the seats in a semicircle so everyone can see the video player easily. This will make transition between the video and group conversation more efficient and natural.

Also, try to get to the meeting site early so you can greet participants as they arrive, especially newcomers. Simple refreshments create a welcoming atmosphere and can be a wonderful addition to a group study gathering. If you do serve food, try to take into account any food allergies or dietary restrictions group members may have. Also, if you meet in a home, find out if the house has pets (in case there are any allergies) and even consider offering childcare to couples with children who want to attend. Finally, be sure your media technology is working properly.

Leading Your Group

Once everyone has arrived, it is time to begin the group. If you are new to small group leadership, what follows are some simple tips to making your group time healthy, enjoyable, and effective.

First, consider beginning the meeting with a word of prayer. Then remind people to silence and put away their mobile phones. This is a way to say yes to being present to each other and to God.

Next, ask a volunteer to read the session's introduction from this study guide to focus everyone on the week's topic. After the "Checking In" time (see below), your group will engage in a simple Bible study called "Hearing the Word" drawn from the content of the video. You do not need to be a biblical scholar to lead this effectively. Your role is only to open up conversation by using the instructions provided and invite the group into the text.

Now that the group is fully engaged, it is time to watch the video clip (approximately twenty minutes; space is provided in the study guide for jotting notes). The content of each *Unfinished* session is deep, so there is built-in time for personal processing before participants are asked to respond to the "First Impressions" question. Don't skip over this part. Internal processors will need the more intimate space to sort through their thoughts and questions, and it will make the "Community Reflection" more fruitful.

Continue with the "Community Reflection" questions. Encourage everyone in the group to participate, but make sure that those who do not want to share (especially as the questions become more personal) know they do not have to. As the discussion progresses, follow up with comments like, "Tell me more about that," or "Why did you answer the way you did?" This will allow participants to deepen their reflections, and it invites meaningful sharing in a nonthreatening way.

Each session features multiple questions. You do not have to use them all or follow along in chronological order. Pick and choose questions based on either the needs of your group or how the conversation is flowing. Also, don't be afraid of silence. Offering a question and allowing up to thirty seconds of silence gives people space to think about how they want to respond and also gives them time to do so.

As group leader, you are the boundary keeper for your group. Please do not let anyone (yourself included) dominate the discussion. Keep an eye out for group members who might be tempted to attack folks they disagree with or who try to "fix" those having struggles. Such behaviors can derail a group's momentum. Model active listening and encourage everyone in your group to do the same. This will make your group time a "safe space" and foster the kind of community that God uses to change people.

"Community Reflection" will be followed by another engagement with the biblical text called "Exploring the Word." Sometimes the Scripture verses are the same as those read in "Hearing the Word" and sometimes they are different. The point of this section is to see how what Rich shared in the video might cast these familiar passages in a new light. Explore any new connections participants might make and resist the desire to resolve any tension they experience while wrestling with Jesus' words. Sometimes that tension is a catalyst for change in someone's life.

The next part of each session is called "Doing the Word," which your group will do together. Take time to read over this section ahead of time, as a couple of the activities require some basic craft materials.

Lastly, a "Closing Prayer" idea is provided to bring your group gathering to an end (sometimes this section is combined with "Doing the Word"). You may follow this prompt or strike out on your own. Just make sure to do something intentional to mark the conclusion of the meeting. It may also be helpful to take time before or after the closing prayer to mention that week's "Living the Word" personal activity (also on a gray background page). Read the instructions before the meeting so you can answer any questions the group might have and thus send everyone out in confidence.

Debriefing

One of the most formative parts of the *Unfinished* experience can be the aforementioned faith experiments, "Doing the Word" and "Living the Word." These activities provide personal opportunities for the participants to connect their everyday lives with the content from the study. After the first week, your group will debrief the previous week's experience during "Checking In" before moving on to the study and video.

Debriefing is a bit different than responding to a video presentation because the content comes from the participants' real lives. The basic questions that you want the group to reflect on are:

- What was the best thing about the activity?
- What was the hardest thing?
- What did I learn about myself?
- What did I learn about God?

Specific debriefing questions have been written for each experiment; however, these four areas are what the "Checking In" time is designed to explore. Feel free to direct it accordingly.

ABOUT WORLD VISION

Who we are

World Vision is a Christian humanitarian organization dedicated to working with children, families, and their communities worldwide to reach their full potential by tackling the causes of poverty and injustice.

World Vision has more than 1,300 staff in the United States, and partners with U.S. government agencies, corporations, foundations, churches, and more than 1.1 million individual donors to help children and their communities overcome poverty and experience "fullness of life," as described in John 10:10. It is the largest member of the global World Vision Partnership, which works in nearly 100 countries through 45,000 staff (around 95 percent of whom are local).

Whom we serve

Motivated by faith in Jesus Christ, World Vision staff serve alongside the poor and oppressed as a demonstration of God's unconditional love for all people. World Vision serves all people, regardless of religion, race, ethnicity, or gender.

How we serve

World Vision has more than 60 years of experience in serving the poor, and works in three key areas—emergency relief, long-term development, and advocacy—to help children and families thrive. In each community where it works, the organization leverages its broad skills and expertise along with its extensive network of global and local partnerships, enabling World Vision to effectively support children's physical, social, emotional, and spiritual well-being.

For more information, go to **worldvision.org.**

You can help:

Want to put your faith into action? Become a World Vision child sponsor and build a friendship with one special child who will know your name, write to you, and feel your love and prayers. Your monthly sponsorship gift will help provide a child and their family and community with sustainable access to life-changing essentials like clean water, nutritious food, healthcare, educational opportunities, and spiritual nurture.

Become a sponsor today at **worldvision.org/sponsorship**

PRES173589_0313 © 2013 World Vision, Inc.

At the author's request, all royalties due to the author will benefit World Vision's work with children in need.

BELIEVING
IS ONLY THE BEGINNING

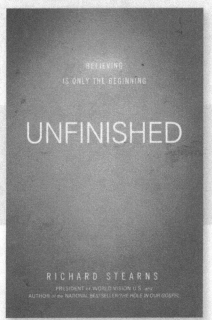

So you believe in God. Now what? What is our purpose and where do we fit in the bigger story that God is writing? How should faith affect our families, our careers, and our money? Why does it all matter? In *Unfinished*, Rich Stearns takes us on a breathtaking journey to rediscover the critical mission of Christ in our world today and the richness of God's calling on our lives.

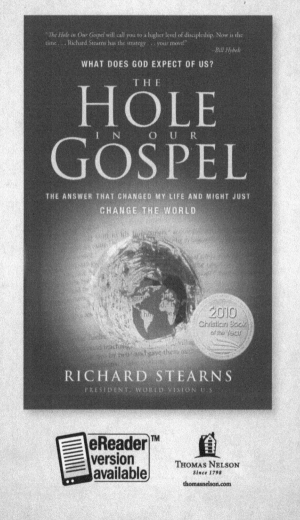

Printed in the USA
CPSIA information can be obtained
at www.ICGtesting.com
LVHW030715050824
787165LV00013B/203